It failed in the USSR... Now it's moved to the USA

SHAKEDOWN SOCIALISM

**Unions, Pitchforks, Collective Greed,
The Fallacy of Economic Equality,
And Other Optical Illusions
Of "Redistributive Justice"**

By OLEG ATBASHIAN

**who saw the worst of both worlds
and lived to tell the tale**

Greenleaf Press, Lebanon TN

Published by Greenleaf Press

www.greenleafpress.com
1570 Old Laguardo Rd
Lebanon, TN 37087

Table of Contents

Preface

Growing up in the USSR, where the only permitted sources of information were textbooks and the official media, I believed that the Soviet Union was the most advanced society in the world. All other countries lived in poverty and oppression, devoid of the sun of Marxism-Leninism. I wanted them to become more like the USSR for their own good, and couldn't wait to grow up and live in the communist future, not worrying about money.

As I grew older, I began to encounter boundaries to intellectual inquiry, coupled with rampant hypocrisy and corruption. I initially attributed these faults to a wrong, dogmatic interpretation of Marxism by the ruling elites. Then came the realization that Marxism was not the solution, but the cause of the dysfunctional system, and that the communist utopia was only a dead-end in humanity's long and stressful journey towards progress. I became an activist, joined the political underground, collected signatures in defense of dissidents, and wrote articles and short stories that satirized socialism and the self-delusional Soviet regime. Most of it was never published.

I moved to the United States in 1994, hoping to forget about politics and enjoy life in a country that was ruled by reason and common sense, whose citizens were appreciative of constitutional rights, the rule of law, and the prosperity of free market capitalism. But what I found was a society deeply infected by the leftist disease of "progressivism" that was jeopardizing real societal progress. So I started writing again, this time in English.

The result is this book, as well as many more essays, political parodies, and cartoons, published in various media in America and around the world. Most of it is collected at my satirical website ThePeoplesCube.com - a spoof of "progressive" ideology, which Rush Limbaugh described on his show as "a Stalinist version of the Onion."

Oleg Atbashian

Chapter 1
Lenin: "Trade Unions
are the School of Communism"

The recent "card-check" debates in the US Congress reminded me of my own experiences with trade unions in the USSR, where organized labor was part of the official establishment and union membership was mandatory. It also reminded me of how that system's seemingly magnanimous goals - fairness, economic equality, and social justice - in real life brought forth a rigged game of wholesale corruption, forced inequality, and grotesque injustice.

Years later, the same Orwellian misnomers are catching up with me in America. One of them is called the "Employee Free Choice Act" - legislation that deprives workers of free choice by replacing private balloting with publicly signed cards in the presence of pushy union organizers. Bad as it is, card-check is only a means to a larger end. Proponents of "redistributive justice" would love nothing more than to use a forced expansion of labor unions as a vehicle to deliver America straight into a utopian swamp, where **they** will gain extraordinary powers while the rest of the nation will be doomed to repeat the Soviet scenario of slow death caused by social, economic, and moral decay.

Defeating the card-check bill alone will not affect the ideology that has spawned it - just as curing a symptom of a disease will not remove the infection. It is the ideology, therefore, that we must address and learn to recognize in its various manifestations.

No matter where I worked in the USSR, I was always a union member without so much as a formal notice -

starting with the student union in college and then on to whatever union was assigned to the state-run enterprise that hired me, regardless of the job description. The only indicators of this one-sided relationship were the monthly union dues, automatically deducted from my measly wages. It was like paying alimony for a fling I never had. To be fair, in the early 80s, I did go on a union-subsidized one-week tour of Uzbekistan - mostly because a friend knew someone at the union office who owed him a favor. But that was it.

Every time I visited a union office in the USSR, I saw the same prominently displayed poster, "Trade unions are the school of communism - V.I. Lenin." At the time it seemed like a sweeping exaggeration, similar to other Lenin gems like "Communism is Soviet power plus the electrification of the entire country," which any student of arithmetic could reformulate as "Soviet power is communism minus the electrification." But recent events in American politics have made me wonder whether the union movement might actually be all that Lenin's quote implies and more - a school, a workshop, and a gateway to communism.

Ideologically, both unionists and communists share the slogan of "economic equality and justice" - two incompatible concepts, given that just rewards make people economically unequal, while forced economic equality leads to great injustice. The pursuit of these contradictory goals in real life results in a dreary outcome. Since absolute equality is unattainable for reasons we will discuss later, forcing it on a society only replaces natural inequality with forced inequality. In this sense, the difference between the two movements is in their radius: communists fancy a forced "economic equality and justice" for all, while the unions limit it to the select group composed of their members.

Strategically, both movements work toward their goals by divorcing wages from labor productivity, stifling the free market, and expropriating and redistributing wealth - all the while blaming the resulting failures and misery on the capitalist "enemy." This can put even non-communist union members in a state of mind that makes them ripe for Marxist propaganda. We can see why Lenin considered communism to be the final destination of the union movement.

In theory, unions become workshops of communism only when they go beyond their original legitimate purpose of collective bargaining and taking care of work-related issues (safety, training, etc.), and turn into collectivist pressure groups that engage in class warfare. In practice, however, there is hardly a union in existence that hasn't become a tool in wealth redistribution schemes that use the "common good" as an excuse for voter fraud, coercion, intimidation, and diverting membership fees to support anti-business policies.

The ultimate result of unions engaging in class warfare was exemplified by the misery of unionized workers in the USSR, who's fleeting desire to be "free from the shackles of capitalist exploitation" led them into permanent slavery at the hands of the state-run economy.

As soon as the factories were turned over to the workers, union perks were reduced to little red flags with Lenin portraits, badges, and honorary titles like "The collective of communist labor." In American terms, that roughly translates into awarding a "Best carmaker of the month" bumper sticker to an auto worker who can't afford a car.

Union perks mean nothing when there is nothing left to redistribute. The Soviets learned it the hard way. The American unions don't seem to be able learn from the mistakes of others. They refuse to admit that their current perks can only exist in a free and competitive economy that ensures growth and generates wealth - also known as "capitalist exploitation" in the lingo of the champions of "redistributive justice." By promoting a state-regulated economy and undermining private businesses whose employees they claim to represent, the unions objectively undercut the workers, who must pay for it with lost jobs and incomes. Setting up the capitalist economy for destruction in this manner qualifies the unions as "the school of communism."

This is not an anti-union argument. To call it anti-union, one has to believe that a union's main purpose is to siphon the nation's wealth to its members. Or that the unions were created to provide logistical support to leftist radicals in their struggle for power.

My argument is quite the opposite: since such overreaching by the unions is self-destructive and ultimately hurts the workers, ridding the unions of inappropriate functions and alliances would benefit everyone - the society, the workers, and even the unions themselves.

The workers are not herd animals, nor are they a separate biological species with a different set of interests. They are as human as anyone else who possesses a mind and free will, and therefore their long-term interests are not different than the rest of humanity. And since the interests of humanity lie with liberty, property rights, and the rule of law, this is what the unions should stand for.

HIGH NOON: 4 June, 1989
Election poster issued by Solidarity Independent Trade Union; Tomasz Sarnecki, Poland, 1989

The shining example of this is Poland's Solidarnosc, an independent union that spearheaded the overthrow of the oppressive communist regime in 1989. Another example can be found in the struggling labor unions of Iran, who oppose the corrupt and oppressive theocracy of the mullahs and could use a little more international solidarity right now, as their leaders suffer beatings, imprisonment, and persecution at the hands of the Islamic Republic's Revolutionary Guards.

Too often, however, unions have blindly taken the opposite side and supported state-enforced redistribution of wealth, forgetting that whenever a government adopts forced economic equality as official policy, unions become redundant and lose not only their political power, but also their very *raison d'être*. That is exactly what happened to the unions in the USSR.

* * *

When Lenin's Party was plotting to take over Russia, it encouraged the unions to engage in class warfare on the Party's behalf and spread the ideas of economic equality and redistribution of wealth. But as soon as the Party was in power, all such activities were discarded. In the words of prominent Party theoretician Nikolai Bukharin, "We asked for freedom of the press, thought, and civil liberties in the past because we were in the opposition and needed these liberties to conquer. Now that we have conquered, there is no longer any need for such civil liberties."

Following the October Revolution in 1917, Russia's former Allies in WWI - France, Britain, and the US - launched a limited military intervention into Russia, seeking to restore the democratic Provisional Government and defeat the communists who had annulled Russia's foreign debt and confiscated private property held by foreign nationals. But the Allies were defeated - not by the Red Army - but by their own labor unions, who launched a campaign of solidarity with "the first workers' state," threatening to paralyze their war-stretched economies. By 1920 the Allies withdrew without much of a fight, and the communists won.

But inside the "workers' state" itself, labor unions were reduced to the position of puppets. Any greater role would have put them in competition with the Party that claimed to speak exclusively for the "toiling masses."

It stands to reason that a state that runs a command economy would subdue the unions and make them a tool of control over the workers. That was why parading the aforementioned quote from Lenin in union offices didn't make sense to me.

The squashing of union power was gradual. For a few years after the Revolution, unions enjoyed some nominal independence. The 1922 labor code closely resembled those in Western countries, while labor productivity remained only a fraction of Western productivity. Sooner or later this contradiction had to be corrected.

The initial understanding was that, because they would be toiling conscientiously for the common good, the workers would become more productive. That never happened. When all the motivational sloganeering, appeals to the workers' conscience, and government mandates to improve productivity failed, the Soviet leaders knew they had hit a wall.

The only variable in this equation subject to the Party control were workers' rights - and they were slashed one by one without so much as a squeak from the unionists who had brought it on themselves.

By the 1930s, the unions were officially absorbed by the state, having become a subdivision of the Labor Commissariat, but without the Commissariat's authority. Most of the labor code had already been rendered obsolete. A single day's absence was punishable by dismissal and, later, by imprisonment.

The state practiced compulsory assignment of graduates to workplaces. Being late for work or leaving early became an offense against the state.

Things kept getting worse, as repression proved to be the only possible way to propel the inefficient state-run economy, with fear and intimidation its only incentives.

By 1940, a worker could no longer resign from a job without the consent of the management, while the state reserved the right to transfer employees at will and without their consent. Local wage increases depended on decisions made in Moscow. The old labor code was removed from usage and no longer published.

A sad joke from that era describes the repressive political climate as follows. Three gulag prisoners are sharing stories of how they got there: "I came to work five minutes late and was accused of sabotage." "I came to work five minutes early and was accused of spying." "I came to work on time and was accused of being a Swiss secret agent." (It was only logical that its own economic inefficiency would lead to official xenophobia - a paranoid cousin of unionist protectionism.)

After Stalin's death in 1953 the terror still lingered for several years. But the reforms of the 1960s brought a new labor code that gave workers more rights than they could remember. And since the unions were now part of the totalitarian state, union membership was automatic and compulsory, with dues automatically deducted from the salary.

Despite the new labor code, the unions never regained independence. Their functions were limited to family care, recreation, and boosting workers' morale. Union functionaries busied themselves sorting out family quarrels, or putting the fear of the Party into philandering husbands and alcoholics who were absent from work for several days but couldn't be fired because unemployment wasn't supposed to exist.

Unemployment benefits didn't exist either. If you didn't have a job the state would find one for you, whether you liked it or not - including sweeping the streets. Since the government owned all industries and services, it could create any number of additional jobs, regardless of economic necessity. Resisting employment by the state was a criminal offense. A brief period without a job was tolerated, but deliberate prolonged unemployment could get one arrested, labeled a "social parasite," and sent off to a labor camp for re-education. The usual suspects were dissidents, vagrants, and dysfunctional alcoholics.

While union representatives were prone to unleash "collective indignation" on "unconscientious" workers, few took their moralizing seriously. In the absence of Stalinist terror as an absolute motivator, the "toiling masses" viewed their relationship with the state as a big joke: "they pretend they're paying us, we pretend we're working." The economy was faltering, causing an even greater scarcity of goods, irregular food supplies, and rising prices.

The only known independent workers' strike in Soviet history happened in 1962 in the Russian city of Novocherkassk. Not surprisingly, the unions played no part in it. It was an unplanned, impulsive outburst caused by the announcement that the government had increased prices on basic food products. Workers at the Electric Locomotive Construction Works were the first to walk out on the job. Most of them were promptly arrested and locked up at the local police station. The next morning, thousands of men, women and children, marched in a column towards the government building to express their demands, and to free the arrested workers.

Bloody Saturday in the Soviet Union
Novocherkassk, 1962

Samuel H. Baron

Khrushchev's relatively liberal reforms hadn't made speaking against the government any less dangerous, but the workers had become too desperate to care. The procession towards the downtown area was mostly peaceful, but random participants reportedly assaulted the Party and KGB representatives who had been trying to stop them, threatening people with retribution. At the same time the demonstrators freely fraternized with the locally stationed soldiers, posted to deny them passage across the bridge.

The frightened officials dispatched ethnically non-Russian special forces who were less likely to mix with the locals, and reinforced them with ten tanks and several armored personnel carriers. In the clash that followed, the soldiers fired at the demonstrators with automatic rifles, killing about 70 people and leaving hundreds wounded. How many were imprisoned remains unknown because the incident was hushed up from the outset, and the convictions were likely veiled as theft, hooliganism, or banditry.

There were no strikes after that for a very long time, non-union or otherwise. Due to the government's total control of the media, no information about the strike and its suppression spilled out of the city limits, let alone into the Western press. The media first reported it during the period of Glasnost in 1989 - twenty-seven years later.

Around the same time, as the hold of the Party was already waning, Soviet coal miners went on a first-since–the-revolution nation-wide strike against the corrupt communist rule - a strike that was not suppressed by the government and widely reported in the Soviet and world media.

Again, unions played no part in it. But they picked up the initiative as soon as they realized the potential power they could wield as strike organizers. As if recovering from a decades-old amnesia, Soviet labor leaders gradually regained the skill of exploiting the workers' anger for political purposes.

After the Communist Party was disbanded in 1991 and the USSR was no more, unions continued with a series of strikes, this time directed against the economic policies of the new, barely hatched independent democracies. Under the guise of caring about the workers, the hard-line communist leadership of the unions did everything in their power to add to the existing havoc, destabilize the new governments, and make the workers plead for the return of the old system.

A post-USSR union poster: "Pay salaries! No layoffs!"
Reminiscent of the Pravda newspaper masthead, this
typeface was popular in the times of the revolution and
later became a staple of the Party's visual propaganda. In
post-communist Russia, it is used subliminally to
manufacture a nostalgic longing for a stern-but-fair Party
leadership with a strong arm and an iron fist, reminding
the workers who their "real defender" is.

ОСТАНОВИТЬ
И НАКАЗАТЬ
СУРОВО
ЛЮБИТЕЛЕЙ
РУБЛЯ
НЕТРУДОВОГО!

Chapter 2
Incoming: Forced Inequality and Economic Injustice

I still lived in Ukraine when the coal miners union in the Donbass region launched a strike demanding higher wages at a time of rapid inflation. This was in the early 1990s, the first years of Ukrainian independence. The timing couldn't have been worse for the barely surviving industries that depended on coal-generated power, as the rest of the country struggled to stay warm in the winter. The miners did get their pay hike. It affected the cost of heating, power, metals, and just about everything else in the country. As the prices went up, the overall gain for the miners was zero but everyone else's lives became even more miserable.

The Donbass miners felt they were cheated and went on another strike. Well-positioned to hold the country by the throat, their union demanded one wage hike after another. The cycle repeated over and over, still leaving the miners with no gain but driving all others, especially the pensioners, into abject privation.

Before long, other unions demanded higher wages, supported by angry workers envious of the "privileged" status of the Donbass coal miners. In an overstretched economy, new pay hikes ended up driving consumer prices through the roof. The wage race was as irrational as cutting a hole in the back of a shirt to patch a tear in the front, but such is the nature of collectivist pressure groups that can't help but fulfill their purpose of extracting privileges for themselves at the expense of everyone else - even in the face of an imminent economic catastrophe.

They got their wish. Soon everyone became a millionaire, walking around with bags full of money because their pockets could no longer hold the huge wads of cash required to buy a loaf of bread, whose cost was now in  the thousands. And even that money they had to spend fast; by the end of the week it was worthless. One of my friends invested part of his rapidly dwindling savings into a pearl necklace for his wife, half-joking that someday they might be lucky to trade it for a warm meal.

We all learned a new word, *hyperinflation*. It equalized everyone, including the Donbass coal miners.

One by one, factories started to shut down. The ones that stayed open began to pay workers with their own products. A neighbor who worked at the knitting factory brought home boxes of socks and stockings instead of money. A mother of two, she spent weeks trying to barter the socks for food and other things her family needed, which made her apartment a "sock exchange" and her a "sock broker." My other neighbor worked at a fertilizer plant; he wasn't so lucky. His plant simply closed. Barter was now the law of the land; people and businesses mostly traded in goods, often in complicated multi-party combinations. But the preferred currency was, of course, the US dollar, which was a sign of progress, given that only a few years earlier, owning "capitalist currencies" would have resulted in a visit from the KGB.

The Donbass coal miners also lost their jobs as their customers either had to shut down or pay them with socks. The little good that came out of their strikes amounted to exposing the philosophical link between trade unionism and communism, and showing why communism doesn't work. It also taught me four things everyone needs to know about inflated union wages, especially those extracted by holding a gasping nation by the throat:

1. Inflated union wages are a form of forced redistribution of wealth. They use government protection to suck other people's money in, without giving anything back.

2. Inflated union wages are futile. They lead to inflated prices; the union members do not become richer but everyone else becomes poorer.

3. Inflated union wages produce an economic monster that ravages the country and eventually consumes its own creators. In richer nations it moves slower due to the abundance of nourishment; in poorer nations it quickly destroys economies, causing massive and unwarranted suffering.

4. Inflated union wages are immoral.

* * *

I now live in the United States, where inflated union wages have already priced the American steel industry out of existence, making the Pittsburgh Steelers an anachronistic reminder of the city's industrial past. Next is the American auto industry, which has become a gigantic union-run welfare agency whose byproduct happens to be automobiles.

An article by Brent Littlefield in *Pajamas Media* describes the reasons: "An unbelievable $1,500 of the cost of each domestic vehicle pays for UAW (United Auto Workers) health insurance. That's more than was spent on the steel. As a result, Americans shop elsewhere: U.S. automakers produce less than 50% of the vehicles Americans now buy."

I have a friend who prices contracts for a construction company in Queens, New York. He uses a computer program that includes an option of cutting costs by decreasing the number of union workers. He applies this option when all the other factors have been computed and the bid needs to go down a notch. If that price wins him the contract, the next step is to bribe the union shop steward at the site. The "shoppie" pockets the money and turns a blind eye to the presence of a few lower-wage non-union workers.

On a construction site at Columbus Circle in Manhattan, an outside freight elevator was built to lift crews and materials. It was operated by an "elevator engineer" who pushed floor buttons at the rate of $37 per hour, competing for the title of world's most expensive bellhop. Two union goons, armed with crowbars, sat at the foot of the elevator all day in lawn chairs, sipping coffee, reading newspapers, or listening to the Howard Stern Show on the radio. Their job was to tell the crews that the elevator was unavailable - at least that's what they told my friend when he needed to lift his workers. But after his boss arrived from Queens with $500 in cash for the goons, the elevator became readily available to their crew for the duration of one week. Thus my college-educated friend learned a new rule of union mechanics: the wheels of a freight elevator needed to be greased for it to appear. This know-how wasn't taught in school, but it appears to be common knowledge on construction sites in New York.

A New York business woman once hired me to design a display booth to be shipped to a conference in Chicago. I also designed her presentations, which we finished on Saturday in her office as she simultaneously did a million other things, impressing me with her ability for multitasking. Her plan was to fly to Chicago on Sunday, set up the booth on the conference floor, hook it up, test the lighting, and show up Monday morning to reap the rewards of meticulous preparation and precise planning. But Monday morning she called me in tears to say that our booth had been vandalized. At the start of the conference she discovered that all the electrical wiring had been ripped out of the panels. A union electrician on the floor half-admitted to his vandalism,

proudly noting that this was a union site and she had no right to plug anything into the wall without hiring a union electrician and paying him the prevailing wage. He shrugged off her argument that she hadn't seen him on Sunday; he didn't work weekends. The union-compliant course of action for her would have been to arrive on a Friday. In

other words, she had to waste two days of her busy schedule stranded in a strange city and pay extra hundreds of dollars in weekend hotel rates, so that a union guy could charge her $50 for inserting a plug into the wall on a Friday.

That certainly made a dent in my prior confidence in the efficiency of the American workforce.

I myself was once threatened by a union agent when I worked for a small Brooklyn-based business involved in reconstruction of New York City public schools. The man called our office demanding $500 to cover the loss in wages for his union. It appeared that our workers had made an opening in the wall for an air duct, then patched it and cleaned up after themselves by collecting the debris into a bucket. Apparently, cleaning up after themselves was a crime; it was supposed to be a union job paid at a higher rate. Our workers broke a sacred rule: no work was allowed unless the unions could use it to squeeze the most out of the employer. I listened as he made his case, then told him to stop being ridiculous and hung up. That triggered a series of angry calls that lasted for several days.

Using expressions that I, a recent immigrant, hadn't yet heard before, the man told me not to mess with the unions and that I didn't know what I was getting into by taking it lightly. I answered that on the contrary, I realized that anyone charging $500 for a bucket of trash had to be a very important man. But I didn't understand why, instead of spending more time carrying buckets, he wasted his valuable minutes on the phone trashing me - a man so unimportant that he took out his own trash free of charge. Every three minutes of the conversation I kept reminding him that he had just lost another $500 in potential wages simply by talking to me. I must have convinced him because the calls eventually stopped.

It was true that I didn't know what I might be getting into. It was later explained to me by an older friend, who was active in the unions back in the 1970s. He recalled how some of the business agents (union organizers) carried guns while visiting private contractors. "They wore suits and during negotiations would occasionally let their jackets open, just enough for a glimpse of the hardware they were carrying. I didn't know of any actual murders, but I knew that uncooperative non-union contractors had their tires flattened, trucks vandalized, and storage buildings set on fire."

"In every election cycle," he further told me, "union members were instructed who to vote for and called upon to volunteer. I supervised crews that made election signs to be installed at the union's direction. Harmless enough, but as a supervisor I learned about what they used to call 'other activities.' That included members going through legal records and files of prison inmates to register felons. Others were checking real estate records, recording people who left the state to replenish the ranks of phantom voters, and using vacant houses as their addresses. Yet others were combing obituaries for the newly deceased. If the quotas remained unfilled, they searched older death records, sending scores of 120 year-old apparitions to vote.

Guess who they voted for?" Sure enough, the candidates have always been pro-union Democrats with an agenda to pay back their benefactors with government pork at the expense of the taxpayers.

My friend assured me that the majority of union members were decent people, but the methods of the union higher-ups included intimidation, coercion, and stealth.

"They tell you what kind of a job you can have and where that job can be. They set the rate of pay and dictate how much you will pay them for the privilege. They tell you who to vote for and are extremely politically active. All in the name of the American Worker."

Eyewitness accounts are supported by mind-boggling official statistics: "In 2005, upwards of 12,000 UAW 'workers' were paid not to work. The Big Three and their suppliers paid billions to keep downsized UAW members on the payroll as part of a UAW contract. One UAW member, Ken Pool, said he would show up to work and then do crossword puzzles. He earned more than $31 an hour, plus benefits. Higher costs and legacy costs for retirees were transferred to consumers."

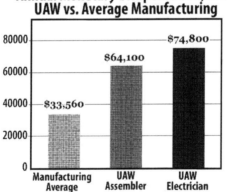

Annual Monetary Compensation, 2006 UAW vs. Average Manufacturing

Having worked in various corporate offices in New York, I noticed a sizeable wage gap between those working in the financial sector and all the rest. Contrary to the caricature portrayal in the media, it wasn't just the CEOs giving themselves bonuses; people on even the lowest levels had higher wages. I understood it as the desire of the financial companies to attract the most capable employees, and as private companies they had every right to do so. What I couldn't understand was a similar gap between the union and non-union workers, who received unequal pay for equal work regardless of their qualifications - a practice the government openly supported and even encouraged by preferential treatment of union contractors in the name of "economic justice."

"Justice" in this case means that non-union employees often work longer and harder while union members enjoy better wages and benefits, as well as job security and other unearned perks. It's even more grotesque once you realize that union perks can only exist on condition that the unprivileged workers of this country and the rest of the world continue to pick up the union tab by paying artificially inflated consumer prices, as their much lower wages help maintain the cost of living at the union employees' level of comfort.

This was exactly what I thought when I observed the sleepy unionized employees at the New York City Housing Authority distributing project documentation to private contractors that was absolutely illegible; it never occurred to them that photocopies should be made from the original sheets and not from the spawn of a hundred generations of copies that were more suitable to conducting Rorschach tests on psychiatric patients.

To compensate for the rigid limitations imposed by the unions, American corporations found a way to retain flexibility by hiring an army of temporary employees through specialized "temp" agencies. I used to be a temp and am describing only  what I saw. The "temps" didn't have the perks of their unionized co-workers, they worked more, and could be fired without warning. For all intents and purposes they were the official second-class citizens of the corporate realm, whose work paid for the privileges of others.

I don't mean to complain; I was grateful for the opportunity to have those jobs, as were most other "temps," and the pay was fair. I felt like a deck boy sailing on luxury cruise ships of socialism that navigated

capitalist waters under the protection of the battleships of trade unions. Unfortunately, there could be no protection against the icebergs of recession and financial crises. And when trouble struck, deck boys got thrown overboard without a life jacket. But capitalism is no more to blame for this than the Atlantic Ocean was to blame for the class divisions among the passengers on the Titanic.

These two unequal classes of employees seem to be a relatively recent byproduct of the policies of "economic equality and justice" - a compromise to avoid death by strangulation as life is trying to wiggle itself out from under the morbid weight of absurd policies. How can such an idealistic goal as forced economic equality create inequality? When the results are the opposite of what is intended, it usually means that the intentions are based on a faulty premise. And since the premise here is "economic equality," it follows that it must be an erroneous concept.

In the same way, on all levels of the economy, unionized socialism has created privileged classes of workers that exist at the expense of the underclass. As such, it has become a parasitic formation that is connected to the capitalist economy the way a parasite is connected to a healthy host body. It would then seem to be in the unions' best interests not to immobilize the host body lest they die along with it.

The paradox of the union movement is that it succeeds as long as it fails to grow. A unionization of the entire country would not only end current exclusive privileges, but would make the economy so stagnant that the ensuing economic crisis would force the government to manage labor relations, restrict union powers, and revise labor contracts. Such a prospect is not so far-

fetched, given the stated government aspirations to regulate paid vacations and sick leaves. This may seem friendly to the unions, but history indicates that when an intrusive government assumes union functions, friendship ends and a competition for power begins, in which the government of course prevails. Having fulfilled their historical mission of advancing a state-run economy, the unions will outlive their usefulness and succumb to the fate of their Soviet brothers as voiceless puppets of tyranny.

And since forced economic equality tends to result in the forced inequality of the authoritarian state, unionized workers will end up being an underclass ruled by the powerful and corrupt state oligarchs, who are the only beneficiaries of a system that redistributes un-earned privileges. If one day union activists wake up under such new management, they will only have themselves to blame.

Chapter 3
Unions: A Study in Collective Greed and Selfishness

American trade unions spent almost a billion dollars in the recent election to put pro-union politicians in positions of power in Washington. The Service Employees International Union, in the words of its own president, has "spent a fortune to elect Barack Obama." According to *The Washington Examiner*, the United Auto Workers had taken a break from bringing the auto industry to its knees and gave $1.98 million to Democratic candidates, plus $4.87 million in independent expenditures to Obama's campaign.

The money came from the mandatory dues of the workers who often wouldn't have donated or voted for these people. In return, the Obama Labor Department is cutting back on the enforcement of federal disclosure rules, without which the workers won't be able to see where their money is going. The union bosses have a very good reason to hide their activities: the AFL-CIO has been spending so much on politics that they're going deeply into debt.

But they are getting the expected payback. The United Auto Workers have been rewarded with owning 55% of Chrysler and 39% of General Motors, with the rest of the shares owned by the Obama government. Let me use the occasion to give Detroit automakers solidarity greetings from the Donbass coal miners. If this trend continues, the younger generation may as well wonder how a town without any motors could ever be called Motown.

When the current recession began, the first weak links
to break in the damaged economy were unionized
businesses - most notably, the Big Three carmakers
dominated by the UAW. By contrast, in the "Right to
Work" Southern states of Alabama, Kentucky, and
North Carolina, non-unionized Japanese and German
carmakers with hourly labor costs 65% lower than those
in Detroit, still continue to employ more than 60,000
American workers without asking for a taxpayer-funded
bailout. And, unlike many of its unionized competitors
that have gone bust, the non-unionized Wal-Mart
remains profitable.

UAW picket line at Star Toyota in Bayside, NY

While the financial crisis itself was not caused by the
unions, it was a product of the same economic

philosophy, which prompted the government to tamper with the housing markets. It started with the desire to help a designated class of low-income families by endowing them with home ownership in the name of "economic equality and justice." But it ended with forced inequality, as countless home loans are now being repaid by taxpayers, many of whom don't even own homes and whose prospects of buying one are getting slimmer as a result.

Solidarity, June 30, 1917. The Hand That Will Rule the World—One Big Union.

The initial market distortion created an economic gremlin - a younger cousin of the Donbass economic monster, if you will - only this time it was strategically placed right in the center of the world's economic engine.

What can go wrong when self-righteous campaigners for economic equality in the government order the banks to issue risky home loans to the poor? Only a ripple effect. The demand goes up, real estate prices rise, chances of repaying the loans get slimmer, the government further pressures the banks to turn a blind eye, the banks begin to repackage bad loans, the bubble bursts, the banks collapse, a recession ensues, borrowers lose jobs and can't afford payments, and the entire financial system goes down. In the worldwide crisis that follows, countless poor people overseas who will never have a house, become even poorer than they were before the US government decided to enforce "economic equality and justice."

Predictably, the fiasco is blamed on capitalist greed and selfishness.

* * *

The word "selfishness" is widely known as a trade-marked fighting word, synonymous with immorality. Leftist ideologues liberally use it to club defenders of capitalism over their ruggedly individualistic heads. However, the same ideologues never decry selfishness when it is practiced by a group - either assuming that selfishness by definition cannot be collective, or that by being collective, selfishness gets an upgrade to a higher moral status, as if things perpetrated in the name of the community cannot be immoral.

And yet, not only has group selfishness always existed on all levels of society - from warring gangs and clans to nations and races - but selfishness exerted by collectivist pressure groups often is the basest, the most irrational and immoral form of selfishness.

While selfishness of an individual can be either rational or irrational, depending on whether it is based on reason or raw emotion, group selfishness is always irrational because crowd psychology is mostly driven by primeval collectivist instincts.

Mussolini was well aware of the power of group selfishness, having built an entire ideology upon it, which he named *fascism* after the symbol of ancient

Roman authority, the *fasci* - a bundle of rods tied together so that they couldn't be broken. In Ukraine where I grew up, folk wisdom summed it up in a sarcastic proverb, "Collectively, even beating up your own father is a breeze."

A moral strength that motivates one to succeed in life through one's own effort and self-improvement can also be described as selfishness. But the collectivists make no distinction between an individual's rational, constructive pursuit of self-interest - and the irrational, destructive selfishness that drives one to sacrifice other people's lives or property for one's own personal gain or to become a leech on society. The two kinds are worlds apart - and yet they are often lumped together, especially when the purpose is the discrediting of successful people and businesses.

The extreme expressions of one's irrational, destructive selfishness - fraud, theft, extortion, and violence - are punishable by law. Society never fails to condemn these actions as immoral, and rightly so. But when the same irrational, destructive selfishness is displayed by a group, it seldom causes the same moral indignation. Likewise, collective fraud, theft, extortion, and even violence don't necessarily result in punishment.

In today's ideological climate, sacrificing other people's lives or property for collective gain, or striving to become leaches on society, is hardly deemed criminal or immoral. On the contrary, group selfishness is being extolled as a virtue and paraded under such euphemistic Orwellian labels as fairness, justice, equality, awareness, and civil rights. According to the collectivist moral code, no sacrifice is too great as long as it is done for the sake of the "many" - even if these "many" are a narrowly defined group with irrational selfish interests seeking to live at the expense of other groups.

In the 20th century, the same moral code inspired communists to sacrifice "some" for the sake of the "many" - with the estimated numbers of "some" ranging from 100 to 200 million people. Nazis used a similar collectivist moral code as they sacrificed millions of innocents to their perverted idea of the "common good," although they could hardly compete with communists in the scale and effectiveness of their "altruistic" efforts.

But even if it hadn't resulted in grotesque mass murder, group selfishness would still be immoral because it dehumanizes people. It denies their unique individuality and alienates them from their human selves. It causes people to be judged, not by the content of their character, but by their color, class, income, ethnicity, sexual preferences, or trade associations. And when these secondary attributes supplant primary human attributes, people cease being individuals and become two-dimensional cardboard cutouts, social functions, sacrificial animals, and expandable pawns in the clash among collectivist pressure groups for unearned status, privilege, money, and power.

In the United States, the corrupting influence of unearned entitlements, fueled by class envy and cultivated grievances, has already recruited enough members to form a solid voting bloc, whose elected representatives never stop trying to legitimize the collectivist new order. The claim on unearned entitlements goes hand in hand with the claim on unearned moral authority - a travesty that few dare challenge. And as the number of unchallenged travesties continues to expand, so does the number of collectivist pressure groups and their appetites.

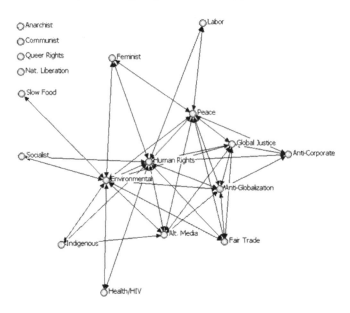

Chart by Department of Sociology and Institute for Research on World-Systems, University of California-Riverside, 2005

Along with *selfishness*, the other popular fighting word trademarked by leftist ideologues is *greed*. Equated with immorality, it is used daily in the left-leaning American media to support a barrage of anti-capitalist arguments.

The American Heritage Dictionary defines greed as "an excessive desire to acquire or possess more than what one needs or deserves." Let's leave aside the subjective word "need," as well as the question "Who defines need?" for another discussion. The key word here is "deserve," which is synonymous with "earn." And while an individual's desire to possess more than what one has earned is being justly condemned as immoral, a collective desire to possess more than what members of a group have earned is becoming increasingly morally acceptable to many Americans, who are now willing to sacrifice their own country to the illusory moral superiority of group interests over individual rights.

At first I was shocked that people as richly endowed with individual freedoms and opportunities as

Americans could fall for such a backward and repulsive social model. But pressure groups admittedly possess a perverse kind of magnetism, similar to that of street gangs, which seem attractive enough for some people to join and forego the chance to advance oneself in the real world.

Membership in a gang gives one the sense of belonging without the requirement of self-improvement. One doesn't need to be an achiever, lead a moral existence, or do anything at all for that matter - all one needs to do is shed his human individuality and not ask questions.

Collectivist pressure groups are all that and much more. They bait people with the promise of instant entitlements just for being a member. Each group has its prescribed role, legend, grievance, and a turf of operations. Each group pulls the blanket of privileges and exclusive rights onto itself, creating new rules and setting up new terms that render the Constitution meaningless. Together, they create an illusion of a vast moral majority, a representative body competing with the US Congress, an alternative government, a massive front battling American capitalism and individualistic civilization.

While any of these groups would more or less fit Lenin's template as "a school of communism," trade unions have been the undisputed pioneers that blazed a trail for the rest of them. Today, they continue to be the most active and powerful players in the system they helped to create.

Postscript: In October of 2009 the Labor Relations Institute, Inc. issued a report containing the following quote:

"ACORN Corruption Ties with Unions and Politics
With the exposure of ACORN's corrupt practices by clever undercover video stings, ACORN's ties to Big Labor have finally made their way into the public discourse. Several congressmen made a presentation in Chicago, making the case that the Census Bureau, who announced they had cut ties with ACORN, should also cut ties with SEIU, as the two organizations seem to be deeply intertwined, both financially

and operationally. Following the flow of funds, another obvious conclusion is that **tax payer dollars doled out to ACORN have also found their way into SEIU coffers, so that non-union tax payers have participated in funding union organizing and political activities.**"

SEIU and the UFCW have been the top financial contributors to ACORN among the Big Labor camp, sending $4,019,606 and $2,189,270 respectively during the years 2005 to 2008. Of the total of $8,618,092 contributed to ACORN by labor unions during this time period, $7,013,081 was attributed to "Representational Activities." A high percentage of union members would be appalled to learn that this is how their dues money has been spent.

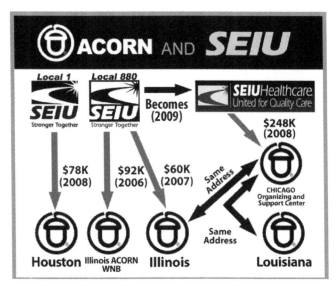

ACORN - SEIU connections
Chart prepared by Illinois Congressmen Mark Kirk and Peter Roskam, with North Carolina Congressman Patrick McHenry, presented at a press conference in Chicago on 9/28/2009.

A Tale of Two Cities

Hiroshima today

Detroit today

*Hiroshima survived a nuclear blast. But Detroit was hit with a much
more damaging weapon; it killed the population's rational faculties
and the very spirit of industriousness that had once made it the auto
capital of the world. The name of this devastating bomb? Union-
favored policies of "economic equality and justice." And there's a lot
more where it came from.*

Chapter 4
Rigging the Economy
in the Name of "Justice"

The demands of forced economic equality are usually justified by the "growing gap" between rich and poor, and men and women, as well as various groups of minorities. Such demands are usually followed by a plan to improve on reality by aggressively tampering with market forces - which, as we already know, can only make the existing income gap worse due to the resulting poverty, economic stagnation, and limited upward mobility.

In a free society, an income gap results from the success of some and the failure of others, and is, for the most part, fair. A rational, constructive way to diminish this gap is to increase the number of successful people by ensuring that everyone has the freedom and opportunity to earn an honest income.

An irrational, destructive approach is to blame the successful, restrict their growth, and redistribute their

property. Its proponents would never call it that, though - they prefer the Orwellian term "economic equality and justice," and sometimes "fairness" for short. Resulting in state-sanctioned inequality, it punishes effort, rewards sloth, fosters corruption, and keeps people down by restricting their freedoms, which is neither just not fair.

That is why the only unfair income gap that deserves to be looked at in today's US economy, is the gap between the market-based, non-union wages and the artificially inflated union wages - a gap that was deliberately created by twisting the arms of businesses, paying off politicians, and lobbying for anti-business regulations.

Observe an absurd charade: union-forced unequal pay for equal work has the blessing of the champions of "fairness" who like to preach equal pay for equal work, while all they really advocate is equal pay for unequal work - otherwise known as the communist principle "from each according to his abilities, to each according to his needs." And these are the same people who can't shut up about the unfairness of capitalism.

They argue that the gap wouldn't exist if all workers joined in solidarity and demanded higher wages, benefits, and job guarantees - or, better yet, elected a government that would force the employers to pay up. Let's test this theory and assume that, as of this morning, all Americans have become equally entitled to union-style wages and benefits. What happens next?

Prices will go up on all essential products. Unionized workers will lose their current advantages. Naturally, the unions will go on strike and use all means in their arsenal to upgrade their members to a "more equal" status. Once they've been upgraded, things will return to the old unequal ways - only now the cost of living will be much higher and people's savings accounts will be severely depreciated. The country will emerge from the pay hikes poorer than before.

And that will only be the tip of the iceberg. The unreasonably high cost of American products will make them less competitive internationally. To maintain a comfortable standard of living in a shrinking economy, Americans will increasingly rely on the influx of cheap products from countries that hadn't been touched by the wage cycle. A skyrocketing trade imbalance will undermine America's standing in the word. A greater number of American businesses will now be outsourcing jobs or hiring illegal migrants in order to stay afloat.

Worsening unemployment, economic recession, and the growing income gap - both domestic and international - as well as the media campaign blaming the crisis on greed, selfishness, and other evils of the free market, will rally more people to the banners of economic equality and redistribution. In the absence of articulate opposition, free enterprise will lose its former attractiveness and Americans will elect a socialist government that will nationalize key industries and begin openly to dismantle the framework of capitalism.

If you find such a dystopia frightening, I have news for you: it is already happening.

"More and more American workers are joining together in unions to claim a share in the prosperity they help to create, while working to improve the services they provide," said SEIU International President Andy Stern.

Engaging in radical politics, the Services Employees International Union (SEIU) has long been taken over by the hard Left. In 2008, this union was more than 88,000 strong.

The deeper we go, the more Lenin's words seem like a prophecy. But there's more. Unions are instrumental in fulfilling yet another of Lenin's directives: "The way to crush the bourgeoisie is to grind them between the millstones of taxation and inflation." And the current US government is going down this path, trying to mend the income gap and the runaway cost of living by increasing the minimum wage. Unsurprisingly, trying to fix an artificially created imbalance by inventing more artificial measures is proving to be as effective as quenching a fire with gasoline.

In the meantime, the self-righteous campaigners for economic equality apply the same approach to narrow the global income gap by sending aid to poor nations - knowing full well that most of it ends up in the coffers of local autocrats whose people continue to live in abject poverty.

Granted, the disparity between rich and poor countries exists to a large extent due to the stark differences in the productivity of labor. But that doesn't tell the whole story. The gap has reached such absurd proportions in large part because the wages inside the industrialized rich nations have been artificially raised to unrealistic heights in the course of repeated, futile cycles of union pay increases, followed by price hikes on most products, with the rest of the national wages trying to catch up.

Who is footing the bill? In an isolated closed system, when things reach a limit of tolerance, the system must either balance itself or break apart. But a country's economy is never a closed system. Western economies are connected to poorer nations, whose lower wages and cheaper raw materials temporarily compensate for the unsustainable costs of maintaining overpaid unionized labor at home.

If poor nations are selling their products at market prices while buying Western products at a price that includes the full cost of the union wages, pensions, healthcare, and other benefits, they are clearly being taken advantage of.

For this they should send their thanks to the campaigners for "economic equality and justice" - who, incidentally, are also the loudest voices in the chorus denouncing rich nations that get richer by robbing poor nations that get poorer.

The tired leftist adage is actually true - but its real causes have nothing to do with imperialism, neocolonialism, capitalist globalization, or any of the other phony labels they fabricate.

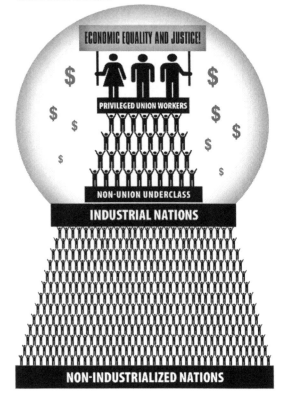

GLOBAL PYRAMID SCHEME:
FORCED "ECONOMIC EQUALITY" RESULTS IN UNFAIR WAGES

The policies of forced "economic equality and justice" create an unsustainable pyramid similar to a Ponzi scheme that unfairly benefits union members in wealthy industrial nations.

As every pyramid scheme, it sooner or later collapses, wrecking entire economies and hurting everyone involved, as well as those who never even agreed to participate in it. The hardest hit will be those at the bottom.

These labels imply that capitalists are deliberately conspiring to promote "unfairness" out of personal greed and selfishness - while their opponents, by virtue of defending "fairness," speak from the position of morality and transparency. But if "moral" is that which advances poor nations and "immoral" is that which inhibits them, then morality is clearly on the side of capitalism. Likewise, if "fairness" means a level playing field, then it entails the elimination of inflated wages and other unearned entitlements, both home and abroad, making all price creation equally transparent.

The expression "level playing field" alludes to the requirement for fairness in games where a slope would give one team an advantage. I am not an athlete; if I play against an NFL professional on a level field, I will lose fair and square. But if we apply the theory of "economic equality and justice" to sports, a fair game would be played if I had a slope and the NFL professional wore foot shackles, while the referee would continually tamper with the scores and rule consistently in my favor. I wouldn't even have to practice, build strength, and learn strategies; the revised rules would already give me a chance to win.

Any sports fan will tell you this is unfair and such rules would be the death of football. And yet, when the same rules are applied to the economy, very few call it unfair or worry about the demise of the market. On the contrary, many agree that this would give someone a mythical "fair chance," although no one knows exactly how or who would be the beneficiary of this.

When the game is rigged, what becomes of its purpose? Who decides what is "fair" and which team is entitled to a bigger advantage? How do we know what bribes are being passed under the table? How can we tell who is a better player or what training, techniques, and strategies are the most effective?

The same questions apply to a rigged economy. Tampering with the market not only breeds economic unfairness, but it endangers the only fair gauge of the true cost of things in the world. Without the open, transparent market, what becomes of the meaning of "fair price"?

In his inaugural speech, President Barack Obama famously declared, "We can no longer afford indifference to suffering outside our borders; nor can we consume the world's resources without regard to effect." I share his concern, but I'm  even more worried that his solution - redistributing unearned entitlements while restraining producers - is what caused the problem in the first place.

The global income gap has already devoured trillions of dollars in foreign aid over the decades, without any sign of improvement. If something isn't working for so long, any rational person would reexamine the theory behind it. Not the champions of equality, however. They continue to demand foreign aid with the moral smugness of someone who owns exclusive rights to the definition of "fairness." But there is a reason why aiding despotic quasi-socialist regimes has never resulted in a prosperous nation.

So far it has only resulted in a bizarre symbiosis between the self-righteous champions of "fairness" in

the West and crooked Third-World authoritarians. The despots long ago figured out that "equality" is a great excuse to violate property rights, "fairness" is a license to abuse the law, "justice" legitimizes dictatorial rule, and "redistribution of wealth" allows looting. They have learned that foreign aid is their reward for doing all of the above while keeping the people hungry.

Robert Gabriel Mugabe, the socialist dictator of Zimbabwe since 1980

It couldn't have happened any other way because the enforcement of all such ideas requires a serious intrusion into the people's lives by the omnipresent state, which also must own all of the nation's resources. This makes any president of such a state the ultimate omnipotent ruler of the land and its people.

Naturally, in the absence of individual rights, opportunities, and the rule of law, the office of "president" becomes a magnet for an endless array of warlords, military thugs, and leaders of nationalistic mobs driven by collective greed and selfishness. Most of these leaders have no idea how to run a country, don't care, and may never have wanted to - if it weren't also a magic key that makes its master the virtual owner of all the foreign aid, gold, diamonds, or whatever else Western geologists can find in the bowels of the state-owned land. This helps to account for the record number of military coups, civil wars, and bloody atrocities happening in the Third World today.

This kind of bloodletting would be greatly curtailed if political elites didn't have control over the ownership and redistribution of the nation's property. Few warlords would want to stage a bloody coup and take over a government whose functions are limited to protecting individual rights and liberties. For that to happen, property must be privately owned by individual citizens and protected by the rule of law from fraud, coercion, violence, and the dictates of the state. Unleashing the powers of capitalism and free markets would make foreign

Idi Amin Dada, *man-eating military dictator of Uganda from 1971 to 1979, demanded that he be addressed as "His Excellency President for Life, Field Marshal Al Hadji Doctor Idi Amin Dada, VC ['Victorious Cross'], DSO, MC, Lord of All the Beasts of the Earth and Fishes of the Sea and Conqueror of the British Empire in Africa in General and Uganda in Particular, and Professor of Geography*

aid unnecessary; it would be replaced by private investments once the opportunities and the rule of law are in place, and a more prosperous population would eventually be able to take care of itself without anyone's help.

But the self-righteous defenders of "fairness" would never allow that to happen. For them it would mean to surrender their "civilizing" influence over the minds of people in favor of "greed," "selfishness," and "evil corporations." It would also entail the loss of their moral authority, and with it, the power to control world affairs, which they presently enjoy.

Note that all the currently warring mobs justify their actions by the desire to take better care of the people, enforce fairness, and improve redistribution. They all use similar quasi-Marxist rhetoric, which has become a prerequisite for the official recognition of a regime by the "world community." Once in power, they spend their days stealing foreign aid, pilfering the country, looting  their neighbors, and fighting off uprisings led by similar thugs who also promise to fight corruption, enforce fairness, and improve redistribution.

A sufficient warning sign that the system is failing is the fact that no foreign-aid-sponsored president steps down voluntarily. The greatest fear of all ex-dictators is to become equal with the people they once "cared about" - poor, powerless, and vulnerable to abuse by any new thug in power.

Granted, "caring" rhetoric as a disguise for abuse and thuggishness is not limited to Third World despots. It exists in any society that accepts rigging the game in the name of "fairness" as its official ideology.

I have seen it in abundance while living in the USSR, but that is what my next chapter will be about.

Chapter 5
Want a Crisis? Impose "Fairness"
I'll See Your Fair Trade and Raise You a Grande Latte

In the early 1990s I worked as a private consultant and interpreter for American business people visiting the former USSR. My employers, many of whom became my personal friends, were looking for business opportunities, which at the time seemed abundant - even to me.

I knew that government corruption existed, but the real scope of the disastrous legacy of Soviet socialism was only revealed to me when our travels exposed me to situations and facts I would not have otherwise known.

To make matters worse, government corruption, incompetence, and the attempts to take advantage of my American friends were disguised with the fig leaf of fairness, caring for the workers, and protecting their wages. It was practically a matter of habit; sometimes I wondered if the crooks themselves knew where the cynicism ended and the caring began.

None of the proposed joint ventures came through because of government officials' absurd demands for kickbacks combined with the requirements of Western-style wages for the workers at a time when the average cost of living in Ukraine was about $50 a month for a family of four. Like children on Christmas Eve, the bureaucrats were holding their breath in anticipation of foreign gifts, exorbitant junkets, no-show jobs, and ready-made factories with salaries equaling those in Europe and the US, without realizing that cheap local labor and low maintenance were their only edge and their only chance in the world economy.

In the meantime, factories continued to close, in part because no one wanted to buy their crude products designed for the Soviet market. The economy was crumbling, half of the country's workforce was unemployed, and even a monthly wage of $50 would have been an improvement, at least until things would pick up.

It was then that we visited the unsmiling woman director of the local sewing factory with a proposal to make jeans from the locally made hemp cloth for a Californian store chain. Keeping a poker face, she gave us a production cost estimate per item that equaled their retail price in an American thrift store. That made no sense, given that in local terms the cost was higher than her average worker's weekly earnings. She was lying and we diplomatically asked her to reconsider. The director, who in Soviet times used to be the equivalent of a US Congresswoman, looked us sternly in the eye and repeated that such was the real cost and it was final. We didn't even get to the part where we could gripe about the quality of her products.

Бдительность
— наше оружие!

At least she didn't ask for a cushy job for her niece right up front like some others did. Every encounter was different; the attitude was almost always the same. One by one the frustrated Americans went home empty-handed, leaving the local officials complaining about the greedy Yankees.

I sincerely hope that the business climate has improved since I left the country. But at the time, the solicitations of kickbacks aside, the indignation at the prospect of capitalist exploitation seemed genuine - at least on the part of former Party bosses.

The gap between Western and local wages was painful and incomprehensible to most Soviets, whom the fall of the Iron Curtain suddenly exposed to the real world. Whatever inequality existed between them and the Party elites was now dwarfed by the wealth of American middle-class visitors. The bureaucrats seemed to resent the fact that private US citizens, obviously standing on a lower societal rung because they didn't hold privileged government jobs, could easily travel around the world, launch projects without any government supervision, act like equals with anyone they spoke to, and pay for a single dinner with a few guests at the local restaurant, costing almost as much as their betters in the local government earned in a whole month.

The money the Americans paid me was a pittance by their standards but it was generous by ours, and I was grateful for it. I didn't hate them because they were "rich"; I was happy for them. They were lucky to be born in a free country that followed a normal path of development fit for human beings. It wasn't their fault that I was born in a country that mutilated itself with inhuman social and economic experiments that made us so poor. America didn't degrade us; our own government did, by throwing our potential into the bottomless pit of an irrational utopia.

The only way to close the gap, I thought, was to abandon the unworkable Soviet system and adopt the American model. It would be a long project but well worth the effort. Certain others believed that the gap should be closed by cutting America down to size. I knew such people; their attitude was a mix of hurt self-esteem, jealousy, and irrational collectivist selfishness, which had been cultivated for generations by the official propaganda. That was to be expected. What I didn't expect was to find a similar attitude inside the United States.

I had previously believed, in my parochial Soviet ignorance, that the spectacular failure of forced equality in my country would serve as a repellent for the rest of the world, making sure that people would stop solving problems by bringing everyone down to the lowest common denominator. Little did I know.

The self-righteous campaigners for "fairness" use a clever trick to advance their ideas. They shock fellow Americans with statistics of how outrageously low wages in the Third World are, without adding that prices on the local markets are low in the same proportion and that people might be able to get by on a dollar a day. That's what my own family's budget was at one time - and we weren't dressed in rags and we didn't starve. Living was cheap as long as one wasn't considering imported goods or foreign travel. Of course, a pair of black market made-in-the-USA Levis equaled a month's wages.

The trick of optical illusion: *The three Lenin figures are of the same size, but their placement out of context of linear perspective is distorting our judgment.*

In the absence of the free market - the only reliable instrument of price creation - prices and wages were determined by the government. Everything was state-subsidized, which may sound like a great idea to all those who don't realize that state subsidies come from their taxes.

The Soviet tax system was a mystery wrapped in an enigma. Under Stalin, taxes were integrated into the state-run economy by default and the workers didn't actually "pay" them. The government simply kept everything according to its needs and gave the workers the rest - just enough to eat and buy simple clothes. On top of that, in the 1960s, Khrushchev introduced a flat income tax of about 10%, which was deducted automatically, without any need to file tax returns. The exact combined income tax was unknown due to a complete lack of transparency, but according to some estimates, it was as high as 95%.

Such camouflaged taxation allowed the official propaganda to describe taxpayer-subsidized services - healthcare, education, and housing - as "free gifts" from the benevolent Party and the government, for which the people had to be eternally grateful. I remember that formulation, taught to me in the state-run school named after V.I. Lenin.

At a closer look, however, the "gifts" turned out to be economic traps, restricting people's choices in healthcare, education, and housing. Even moving to another city was an almost insurmountable problem.

СПАСИБО РОДНОМУ СТАЛИНУ,

ЗА СЧАСТЛИВОЕ ДЕТСТВО!

Such government "largesse" turned people into slaves of the state. Little wonder it resulted in a Third-World-type poverty.

But the international income gap is not set in stone. When some Asian countries admitted that their poverty was the consequence of archaic political and economic systems, they remodeled themselves and embraced capitalism. It caused a torrent of sob stories in the Western media, in which well-paid journalists championed "economic equality and justice" by accusing local and Western entrepreneurs of running sweatshop economies. Armies of smug armchair egalitarians participated in well-funded, professionally orchestrated boycotts against companies like Nike that dared build factories in the area and give jobs to poor Asian families.

It almost seemed as though they didn't like the fact that the Asians made an effort to improve their lot instead of begging and demanding aid from richer nations like the rest of the Third World did. But the Asians knew better. Today, such formerly poor countries as Hong Kong, Singapore, and South Korea enjoy median household incomes that are twice as high as those in the former Soviet Republics, which continued to protect their labor. They achieved it, not by accumulating grievances and demanding entitlements, but by releasing their potential through free enterprise and technological advancements. And others are on the way.

Even the Chinese communists have come to the realization that, instead of exporting the "workers' paradise" they would be better off exporting consumer goods. Seeing that their experiments in "fairness" resulted in disastrous poverty, they scaled back forced equality and jump-started a new semi-capitalist economy by entering into a symbiotic relationship with the arch-capitalist America. The last thing China needs right now is for the US to turn into a China, which would be a giant step backwards for both nations.

In the past, Marxist state-run economies had to rely on capitalist free markets to determine the true cost of their own products. Today, as major capitalist economies themselves are falling under the spell of anti-market regulations, the true cost of their own products is also becoming unclear, causing an unsustainable growth of wages and cost of living. This leaves the least regulated economies of the upstart capitalist nations as the only reliable gauge of the true cost of labor and products.

ThePeoplesCube.com

The more realistic foreign wages may seem scandalously low to Americans who don't cringe at $4 for a Grande Caffe Latte. Quite a few of them enjoy sitting at Starbucks in the company of like-minded comrades - each holding a cup of overpriced fair-trade-certified coffee - and complaining about the "unfairness" of this economy, the income gap, big corporations taking advantage of low-wage foreign laborers, and the outsourcing of American jobs. They would surely be surprised to learn that the amount they're paying for one Grande Latte may actually be the true cost of their own day's work and in a truly fair economy, it would also be a fair daily wage.

But they could still go to Starbucks - in a fair economy, a cup of coffee might also cost about ten cents, in addition to a forty cent lunch. And - best of all - low domestic wages would bring those outsourced jobs back!

They might be even more surprised to learn that the "evil" corporations are their best allies. Both politically and culturally, the big corporations are some of the biggest champions of state-regulated entitlement programs and labor wage hikes, thus making the $4 coffee at Starbucks affordable to the masses.

Proponents of forced economic equality like to explain corporate support of government entitlements as evidence that such programs are actually good for business - otherwise why would these "mega-monsters of predatory capitalism" encourage entitlements?

But the truth is much more cynical. Anti-market measures give big companies an unfair advantage over smaller competitors and upstarts who can't afford to have a lobbyist in Washington, and who will choke on higher wages, taxes, and entitlements. Large corporations can swallow the extra cost more easily, as economies of scale allow a smaller price increase on their products.

Corporations are neither demons nor angels - they are merely playing by the rules given to them by the government, which keeps "correcting" the playing field to make it more "fair" by inventing new rules and tampering with the score in the middle of the game.

The rules may be always changing, but the goal does not. And the primary goal of any business organization is profit. So the players must keep adapting to the changing field conditions in order to benefit the shareholders. And if trying to make the best of a rigged game is turning them into monsters, the fault is not so much with the players as with those who have corrupted the game by rigging it.

So the next time a proponent of "fairness" gripes about the rich getting richer and the poor getting poorer, we should agree wholeheartedly - adding that the reasons for the shrinking middle class and the stagnant economy are government regulations born of the dream of forced economic equality, which in real life results in a rigged game, arrested upward mobility, and a more rigid class structure.

The same argument applies to the champions of forced global equality. Since the productivity of labor cannot be made equal globally, the only option within their reach is a global equalization of wages, which they see as a variable they know how to control. Some have made careers out of it.

Instead of leveling the playing field by reducing the government dictate, and by promoting liberty, opportunity, and property rights in developing nations - which is the only fair, realistic, and moral solution to poverty and stagnation - the collectivists are now proposing the imposition of a global minimum wage.

This is as practical as legislating greater rainfall in the Sahara Desert, or establishing international quotas on floods, pestilence, and volcano eruptions. The only thing that is certain to start growing as a result of this measure will be the power of the coming global government, whose first major task will be to tackle a self-inflicted global crisis.

Chapter 6
The Fallacy of
"Economic Equality"

On the surface, the idea of economic equality may seem like an honorable moral goal, which explains its resilience and attraction. This is why it continues repeatedly and with impunity to bring one economic and social disaster after another anywhere it's tried. On the flip side, opponents of economic equality are branded as greedy, selfish, and immoral - which is why few politicians dare oppose this absurdity.

The current political debates mostly end up in the following compromise: capitalism may be more economically efficient, but it's still morally inferior to economic equality that benefits most people. Such a view has two big problems.

It is, in fact, efficiency that benefits most people by raising living standards, reducing the number of workers involved in low-paying and tedious manual work, increasing the number of well-paid intellectual jobs, continually improving everyone's quality of life, and giving the poor access to things that only the rich could enjoy only a short while ago. Therefore, efficiency is moral - and, as such, it renders the above formula invalid.

But let's assume for the sake of argument that economic equality is also efficient, so that we could leave this part out and compare what's left. The resulting picture still can't withstand moral scrutiny.

Since economic equality cannot be attained by bringing everyone up to the level of the achievers, the achievers will have to be brought down to the level of mediocrity, with most of their earnings and property taken by the government. Even the most "progressive" achievers wouldn't submit to this voluntarily (see Hollywood tax returns), so it has to be a forced measure. To do this on a national scale, the state must assume supremacy over private citizens and limit certain freedoms. What's more, forced extraction and redistribution corrupts the government by giving it arbitrary powers to determine various people's needs, for which there can be no objective standards. Most bureaucrats are not paragons of honesty. Even if they were, in due course idealists will become replaced by eager crooks seeking to distribute entitlements in exchange for kickbacks. And finally, such a system corrupts the very people it intends to help, by demeaning the individual productive effort and encouraging a destructive collective scuffle for unearned privileges among pressure groups driven by greed and selfishness.

These are the reasons why all attempts at forced economic equality have always resulted in corruption, poverty, oppression, and moral degradation. What honorable and moral idea  would bring such results? What honorable and moral idea would require a blind, endless sacrifice of people's work, careers, ambitions, property, and lives, to an unattainable utopian goal that, at a closer look, isn't even a virtue? The only way economic equality can benefit most people is by satisfying their class envy.

Some people understandably fear the uncertainty of outcome of their daily efforts, seeing it as a dangerous void separating them from a safe and comfortable future. A rational reaction to this would be to remind oneself that, ever since people lived in caves, nature has never offered us certainty, and that risk-taking, combined with intelligence and creativity, has built modern civilization - which may be imperfect, yet it's as good as it gets historically in terms of comfort and safety for those participating in it.

An irrational reaction would be to panic, take offense, become impatient with the world, and join a self-righteous political cult that promises a guaranteed certainty of results on the other side, just as soon as they fill the void in front of them with other people's property and the dead bodies of those who dare stand in the way of their brazen march toward the bright future.

The problem with this plan is that the void has no bottom. Enormous wealth is known to have disappeared in it without a trace, along with many people's dreams, aspirations, and entire lives. And even if it could be filled, against all laws of nature and economics, what kind of monsters do we expect to enjoy walking over this smoldering mass grave and be happy on the other side of it? What does it say about the moral character of the champions of this plan?

* * *

A complete economic equality is unattainable. Since all of us have different talents, experiences, knowledge, skills, ambitions, and physical characteristics, the only way to make us equal is to bring us down to the lowest common

denominator. Besides the fact that it would make everyone unhappy, jealous, hateful, irritated, and suspicious of each other's motives and achievements, it is also humanly impossible to enforce. If that were to happen, musicians would need to have their fingers broken to compensate the non-musicians. Alternatively we could issue government quotas for the tone-deaf minority to be included in all musical performances, while forcing all the others to appreciate their tunes under the threat of punishment. Or we could simply ban music.

If some people had wings and others didn't, and the government wanted to enforce "fairness," soon no one would have wings. Because wings cannot be redistributed, they can only be broken. Likewise, a government edict cannot make people smarter or more capable, but it can impede the growth of those with the potential. Wouldn't it be fair if, in the name of equality, we scar the beautiful, cripple the athletes, lobotomize the scientists, blind the artists, and sever the hands of the musicians? Why not?

Back in 1883, a Yale professor, William Graham Sumner, brilliantly addressed these issues by explaining why the real progress of civilization is attained, not by re-distributing wealth, but by expanding economic op-portunities and ensuring people's liberty to earn their own wealth. And since some will always profit eagerly from the opportunities while others will neglect them altogether, the greater the freedom and opportunity in a society, the more economically unequal the citizens will become. "So it ought to be, in all justice and right reason," said Sumner.

"The yearning after equality is the offspring of envy and covetousness," Sumner wrote in his book *What Social Classes Owe to Each Other*. ". . . there is no possible plan for satisfying that yearning which can do aught else than rob A to give to B; consequently all such plans nourish some of the meanest vices of human nature, waste capital, and overthrow civilization. But if we can expand the chances we can count on a general and steady growth of civilization and advancement of society by and through its best members. In the prosecution of these chances we all owe to each other good-will, mutual respect, and mutual guarantees of liberty and security. Beyond this nothing can be affirmed as a duty of one group to another in a free state."

Already back then, Sumner's views were opposed by the self-described "progressives." Today, more than 130 years later, their spiritual heirs have finally gained enough power and moral authority to remake the nation and to slice and distribute the stolen American pie to collectivist pressure groups.

Ironically, they couldn't have done it without all the real progress America has achieved despite their efforts. And, as the campaigners for economic equality are dismantling civilization, wasting capital, and regressing to the archaic tribal mentality, they insist on calling it "progress."

They also insist that they are doing it "for the children," which is going to be the subject of the next chapter.

Chapter 7
Joyriding the Gravy Train
of Economic Inequality

Let us imagine a utopian country named Sovdepia, whose people love the children so much that they voluntarily agreed to redistribute all their material wealth equally to level the playing field for future generations. Let's further imagine that a few years later we visit Sovdepia on a taxpayer-funded fact-finding mission.

Upon arrival, we are surprised to see how little material equality is left, especially among the children. We find local social scientists and ask them what happened. They sadly point at the differences in the Sovdepians' habits, virtues and vices, ambitions, health, and plain dumb luck. But the most powerful reason for inequality, they tell us with dismay, turns out to be the highest Sovdepian virtue - the unconditional love of the parents for their children and the desire to do the best for them.

The truth is, even the most hardnosed Soviet ideologues still cheated the system when it came to their offspring. Having risked life and limb fighting for universal equality, they all ended up inventing creative workarounds to make their own children "more equal" than others. Who can blame them? They were human, even if they denied humanity to everyone else. And who can blame Barack Obama for sending his two daughters to an expensive private school? He only wants the best for his children, even if he is promoting the inferior public school system for everyone else's.

No parent, including the politicians who are forcing economic equality on Americans, will deny their own children added privileges that come with government positions. Anything less would be heartless and uncaring, even if it would contradict their life-long battle against the "heartless and uncaring" opponents of economic equality, which they themselves will be now violating. Given that parents will always be in different positions to endow their offspring, the next generation following any hypothetical Great Redistribution of Wealth will grow up economically unequal. Only this time, in the absence of freedom and opportunities, their wealth and privileges will be largely unearned. And that will finally give the "yearning after equality" the moral validity it badly lacked before.

But until such time, while equal freedom and opportunity still exists, the only justification for the forced redistribution of wealth is class envy - an emotion based on a subjective perception of other people's wealth regardless of how it was earned. And the relative and subjective nature of wealth makes the case for its redistribution even flimsier.

Consider the fact that the Soviet apparatchiks, smugly driving their Volgas past the average Soviet pedestrians, themselves looked pathetic next to American middle-class families, with Chevrolets in the front and swimming pools in the back of their suburban houses.

The apparatchiks liked to be called "people's servants." Unlike their less equal "masters," they were allowed to travel to the West. The striking material contrast must have caused many of them to entertain a criminal thought that, were they to discard their own system of government redistribution and give people the opportunity to earn real income without government obstruction, everyone's living standard would quadruple - including their own. But since in a free and competitive society they wouldn't be the ones with the most power and privilege, the certainty of smaller unearned rewards outweighed for them the opportunity to earn greater rewards with honest efforts. So they continued to "serve" the people by keeping them down and staying on top.

Observing the class-envy mentality on both continents, I noticed a recurring pattern: other people's wealth always appears larger and irritates more forcefully at a closer distance. Since envy is based on emotion rather than reason, one's personal perception of a wealthier neighbor is more unsettling than some distant, greater wealth measured on an abstract absolute scale, which can only be perceived by reason.

The reverse side of the class-envy mentality is the notion that being better off than your neighbor is more satisfying than being wealthy by absolute standards while knowing that your neighbor still has more. The folk wisdom of my home country put this in a story: a king promised a peasant that he would grant him any wish on condition that his neighbor would get twice as much. The peasant laughed and asked the king to poke him in one eye. In another tale a man who could wish for anything, wished that his neighbor's cow were dead. And so on.

An historical comparison makes the relative nature of wealth even more obvious. While today's poor people may seem poor compared to their middle-class neighbors, on an absolute scale they are better off than the rich people in the days of William Graham Sumner.

Not only do they have better medicine, longer life expectancy, running hot and cold water, electricity, gas stoves, and indoor plumbing - they have what even the richest and the most powerful people on earth couldn't dream of - camera cell phones, digital players, air conditioners, refrigerators, microwaves, TVs with hundreds of channels for entertainment, video games, DVD players, fast and comfortable cars with music and AC, air travel, and computers that can instantly connect them with anyone in the world.

Consider the possibility of never having progressed to this level.

For instance, if today's labor laws were to be enforced prior to the Industrial Revolution, machines would not be allowed to replace the workers, and so most of them would be until this day engaged in mind-numbing manual labor. We would still be living in a pre-industrial society, with a handful of aristocrats and the vast majority of poor people toiling with hammers and sickles, living in filth, losing half of their children at birth, and dying at 40 because there would be no medical equipment and mass-produced drugs.

The Soviet Union's backwardness was caused, not by the lack of ingenuity of its people, but by the counterproductive economy of state-regulated social-ism. Without capitalist achievements to learn from and copy, the USSR would have remained perpetually stuck in the 1930s. And so would the United States, if the American "progressives" who opposed Sumner were to get the upper hand a century ago and halt the development of capitalist entrepreneurship. In that case, the few remaining rich people in America would be living blissfully unaware of the unfulfilled possibilities of the 21st century, where even the poor could have had a better quality of life.

Likewise, today's rich people, with all their combined wealth, can't buy the material goods and the quality of life that will likely be available to the poor of the next century. Technological progress is known to have that democratizing effect. And the poor - whatever this word will mean a century from now - are likely to continue to

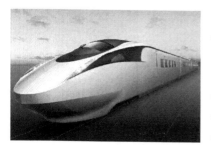

enjoy free rides on the gravy train of capitalist innovation and mass production, unless the current trend towards class envy and forced economic equality stops this train in its tracks. That would bring everyone down, but the poor - to borrow a "progressive" media cliché - the poor will be hit the hardest.

Thus, class envy is an unmistakably irrational impulse. And since the demands for economic equality and redistribution of wealth are the derivatives of this impulse, they are just as irrational, unsupported by reality, harmful, and immoral as class envy itself.

The very notion of economic equality implies that our lives are determined solely by material factors and that nothing spiritual matters. Granted, human dignity requires a certain minimum of material comfort. But once we are above that threshold and still continue to measure our dignity and our entire existence by the level of material comfort, we are, by implication, degrading free will, intellect, liberty, opportunity, and the greatness of the human spirit. This is an ugly distortion of human nature, to put it mildly. It is this philosophical view that allows the "progressives" to excuse skyrocketing crime by pointing to the "poverty" of its perpetrators, despite the obvious fact that no hardship during previous generations ever produced such an obscene crime rate.

After visiting a government housing project in the Bronx, P. J. O'Rourke commented that he himself had grown up in a poor home with a single working mother, among children who wore patched, faded, but neat clothes  inherited from older siblings or neighbors. Most of them turned out well and succeeded in life. That was poverty, he writes. But this - $200 sneakers, gold chains, used condoms and needles in a dirty, urine-soaked stairwell with broken windows - this is not poverty, this is "something else."

This "something else" is precisely the consequence of the view of human beings as spiritless creatures, devoid of mind and free will, and dependent on the government for sustenance. It also happens to be a view that permeates today's media coverage of domestic and international events, as well as films, books, and TV shows produced by cultural elites obsessed with economic equality.

Few of them will argue that the spiritual rewards one derives from life are often more important than the material ones, and that a poor artist may enjoy a richer spiritual life than a government clerk or a CEO. But doesn't that make them spiritually unequal? Shouldn't cultural elites make award-winning movies and documentaries exposing an appalling spiritual unfairness? Shouldn't they call for massive street protests against the poor artist - the metaphysical hog who selfishly hoards spiritual values and leaves others to live in moral depravity? Shouldn't the clerks and the CEOs use media channels to vent their spiritual envy, decry the spiritual gap, and give scripted media interviews about the indignity of living in a system that allows the rich in spirit to get richer as the poor in spirit get poorer? Where are the self-righteous campaigners for spiritual equality?

Let us defer these questions to the experts on "egalitarian justice," whose one-sided fixation on economic equality can be explained by the fortunate circumstance that spiritual equality is beyond their control, or they would be redistributing that as well. Not that they haven't tried to redefine spirituality, supplant it with a surrogate version, and preach the redemption of guilt for having a bourgeois lifestyle. The redistribution of surrogate spiritual units in the form of carbon offsets payable to the Church of Climatology is one of the recent additions, along with the new definition of original sin as "having been born as a carbon-based life form."

The only kind of equality that can be realistically achieved among humans is equality before the law, meaning equal rights and opportunities for all. Despite some historical setbacks, such equality has already been achieved in the Western world, and its beneficial results are obvious. Equality before the law is incompatible with forced economic equality, which rigs the game by infringing on the rights of the more productive in favor of the less productive, limiting opportunities for some to benefit others, and taking by force from one select group only to give unearned material gains to another select group.

To summarize, state-enforced redistribution of wealth in the name of economic equality will always split society into two unequal classes - the corrupt autocratic elite and the powerless majority, impoverished by economic stagnation. Its utopian goals notwithstanding, the main characteristic of such a society is forced inequality. In order to function, the state must stifle dissent and subordinate previously independent institutions that helped to erect the collectivist edifice, such as the media, trade unions, trial lawyers, and other special interest groups. All special interests are superseded by the interests of the state, represented by an authoritarian leader.

The only real choice before us, therefore, is not between economic inequality and economic equality, but between two types of economic inequality.

One is the transparent, volunteer economic inequality of laissez-faire capitalism, where people are free to choose opportunities that they like - but that also lead to predictably different compensation. Whether it's the intense life of a CEO taking risky decisions, or the safe  but uneventful existence of a government clerk, or the relaxed bohemian lifestyle of an artist - these are free choices based on what best suits people's character and makes them happy, taken with full knowledge of the potential risks and rewards. The CEO, the clerk, and the artist receive different compensation for their work, yet they are all equal before the law, which protects their contracts with society and with each other.

These are not rigid classes; people can change their lives if they want to, and their children do not have to follow in their footsteps if a certain lifestyle or profession does not match their idea of happiness. Their material rewards are just since they are determined by the free market, and the differences motivate everyone to be more creative and productive. This system has brought prosperity, opportunity, and happiness to most people, making them equal beneficiaries of liberty and human dignity, as long as they don't succumb to crime, drugs, or class envy.

The other type of economic inequality is the state-enforced redistribution of wealth, which is never transparent. The only successful career in such a system can be made inside the state hierarchy, which sooner or later becomes a snake pit ruled by cronyism, nepotism, kickbacks, and backstabbing.

Cartoon by Victor Vashi, from *Red Primer for Children and Diplomats*, 1967

Given the existence of two distinct and unequal classes, the citizens face only two basic choices: to be a silent slave of the corrupt establishment, or to join the establishment and climb up the career ladder towards the unearned rewards and further away from the faceless, "less equal" masses below. Equality before the law ceases to exist, along with individual choices, aspirations, dignity, opportunity, and liberty - all sacrificed to the utopian illusion of "fairness." As a result, neither the masses nor their rulers are happy with their lives.

Cartoon by Victor Vashi, from *Red Primer for Children and Diplomats*, 1967

Some years ago I escaped from the shipwreck of the Soviet "workers' paradise" and moved to the United States, making a conscious choice between the forced inequality of socialism and the volunteer material inequality of capitalism. I didn't expect to be rich; I only wanted an opportunity to earn an honest income without sacrificing my dignity. I wanted the freedom to pursue my own choices and aspirations, not the ones prescribed by the state. I wanted to live in a country where my success or failure would depend on my own honest effort, not on the whim of a bureaucrat. I wanted my relations with people to be based on voluntary agreements, not mandatory requirements. And finally, I wanted my earnings to be protected by law from wanton expropriation.

America deserves credit for living up to the ideas of liberty and fighting off the redistributionist utopia for as long as it has. As crippling as the hosting of two opposing economic systems can be, it still remains a free country. But the balance is rapidly changing. Like many immigrants seeking freedom and opportunity in America, I find this change not simply misguided but personally painful. And so do all freedom-loving people elsewhere in the unfree world, for whom the mere existence of this country still gives hope and validates their belief in liberty and individual rights.

A False Image of Capitalism
Doesn't Survive the Test of Time

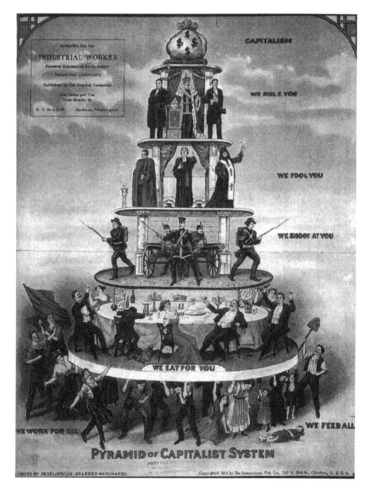

Note how archaic and foolhardy these notions appear today in free-market economies, where common workers have access to more and better goods and services than those at the top of the pyramid at the time.

The depicted rigid social structure and lack of upward mobility belong, not to capitalism, but rather to an aristocratic feudal society. This "progressive" drawing may have been an ambitious attempt to condemn capitalism in 1911 when it was created, but after a century of real capitalist progress it looks more as a mislabeled snapshot of a bygone era.

More precisely, the drawing reflects a time in European history when the elements of capitalism were gradually penetrating the old feudal system and transforming it from within. Today it's the socialist elements that are penetrating and transforming the capitalist system, bringing back the same pyramid they purportedly want to destroy.

But can such a pyramid exist today? Yes it can! With minor adjustments it is a fair representation of life in the socialist "people's republics" of Cuba, North Korea, and all those nations that rejected capitalism as an economic model.

It surely reminds me of the Soviet system with the majority of the people at the bottom, the feasting apparatchiks above them, followed by the KGB, the Party propagandists, and the Party and state elites at the top, with the pinnacle made of collected works by Marx and Lenin.

I hope you enjoyed this book. It was written in response to a great number of emails sent to me by readers after Pajamas Media published my earlier essay about the similarities between Obama's and Stalin's methods of pitting unions against businesses. I thought it would be fitting to include that essay in an appendix.

- Oleg Atbashian

Maksim - ThePeoplesCube.com

APPENDIX
Obama the Pitchfork Operator:
Remake of a Soviet Classic

While some of today's comparisons between Obama and communist dictators may go over the top, the general direction of such thinking is not without merit: they share a utopian goal of forced equality. It's logical then to expect that their methods may also converge at some point. To wit, recent actions from Obama reminded me of a ploy Stalin used on Western entrepreneurs, which in itself is an illustrative morality play contrasting the differences between socialism and capitalism.

"My administration is the only thing between you and the pitchforks," Barack Obama told the CEOs of the world's most powerful financial institutions on March 27, when they cited competition for talent in an international market as justification for paying higher salaries to their employees.

Arrayed around a long mahogany table in the White House state dining room, the bankers struggled to make themselves clear to the president, but he wasn't in a mood to hear them out. He interrupted them by saying, "Be careful how you make those statements, gentlemen. The public isn't buying that."

To get the full flavor of the president's implication we must remember that in Obama's code language, the word "pitchforks" means "a vigorous campaign of threats and intimidation perpetrated by Obama-sponsored ACORN and union activists in conjunction with theatrical outrage from government officials, amplified by the complicit media, and coordinated from one political center, which has now moved to the White House."

Accordingly, the words "public" and "the people" denote "an appearance of broad popular movement created by a small but highly organized band of professional pitchfork operators (ACORN) who rely on the government funding and the media's eagerness to present their deliberately planned actions and pre-fabricated messages as heartfelt and spontaneous."

In compliance with Orwellian logic, Obama's "Newspeak" not only redefines existing meanings, it also abolishes ranges of "Oldspeak" meanings such as property, markets, competition, capitalism, political opposition, and the rule of law. The latter is perhaps the most important ingredient missing in his new "pitchfork" formula, signaling that law is now being replaced with mob rule.

In a balanced society, an angry mob is never a part of the equation. But if the goal is to throw a capitalist society off balance in order to change it, an angry mob is the ticket. Anger is known to be the easiest and the most effective tool of crowd manipulation. Angry mobs  cancel out the rule of law. Infusing anger into a community and turning it into an angry mob, canceling out the rule of law, and changing the balance in a society - this is what community organizers do for a living.

It was often pointed out during the election that Obama lacked management experience. While having a president with no experience is bad, it's not nearly as bad as having a president with experience as a community organizer.

Community organizers were instrumental in forcing banks to give subprime loans to unqualified minority borrowers by using the "pitchforks" tactics - protesting in front of the banks, camping on the lawns of the bankers' family houses, intimidating families, and suing in courts. After the bankers were sufficiently roughed up, a community organizer would show up at their office to "negotiate" the bank's surrender in the form of bad loans and money for community organizations that pay community organizers for their "services."

> BE CAREFUL HOW YOU MAKE THOSE STATEMENTS, GENTLEMEN. I'M THE ONLY THING BETWEEN YOU AND THE PITCHFORKS.

Squeezed between the "pitchforks" and the government (see Community Reinvestment Act), the banks survived by releasing the accumulated toxic assets to the rest of the financial system, which over the years poisoned the entire world economy. Now that the crisis has propelled a former "pitchfork operator" into power, it shouldn't surprise anyone that the new organizer in chief would try to "heal" the economy how he knows best: by continuing to squeeze businesses between the "pitchforks" and the government - a tactic that had caused the disease in the first place. Only now he is doing it on a global scale.

Once a community organizer gains control of the media and the government, the next logical step is to turn the entire nation into a mob and set them against businesses, while offering the latter government "protection." The subsequent takeover of the economy leaves the future society reduced to the two basic elements: an authoritarian government and a compliant mob. This may be an ideal arrangement for a community organizer, but it's a direct opposite of what the Founding Fathers had intended.

Most Americans will probably associate this trend with the protection racket that was rampant in Chicago in the 1930s. It follows the same pattern: the mob, in conjunction with the unions, would organize strikes and protests, do physical damage, and intimidate business owners. Then a mob representative would meet with the owner and offer "protection" by saying "I'm the only thing between you and the pitchforks."

Curiously enough, at about the same time, a similar drama was unfolding halfway across the world in the Eastern Siberia - only this time the role of the mob was played by a government that claimed to act in the interests of the workers. And while the mobsters were motivated by greed and used the workers simply to milk the capitalists, a workers' government, motivated by the common good morality, used the workers for something much more sinister and immoral.

After the Communists nationalized Siberian gold mines, the government's incompetence and lack of incentives sent gold production into a decline. Many of the managers and engineers had fled abroad; the foreign-made mining equipment lay in ruins. But the country badly needed gold to finance industrialization and prepare for war with Western capitalism.

The popular sentiment, whipped up by the party-controlled media, was that "heads must roll." Failing to deliver the required quotas, the remaining managers and engineers were declared enemies of the people and either executed or sent to hard labor camps. That didn't help; the production continued to drop.

That's when Nikolai Bukharin, a former community organizer in charge of industrial development, came up with an idea to infuse some capitalism and lease Siberian mines to British mining companies. The plan was approved by Stalin.

ON TOP OF LENIN'S TOMB, 1929
BUKHARIN   STALIN

The lease terms were extremely favorable; before long British capitalist exploiters arrived at a few Siberian locations. They brought new equipment, trained the local workers, and quickly revived the industry. But as soon as things began to run smoothly, local unions organized strikes at all British-run mines, protesting exploitation and demanding a significant pay raise.

The strike sounded absurd as the miners' wages and living conditions by then were among the best in the country. The foreign management didn't realize, of course, that the strike had been secretly ordered by the party's central committee as part of Bukharin's clever scheme. The unions wouldn't dare defy the party. The workers simply did what they had been ordered to do.

The British gave in and raised the wages. But a few weeks later another strike broke out, with more picketing and demonstrations, as the unions demanded another significant raise and improvement of living conditions. The British gave in again. After yet another strike the Siberian miners already had a higher living standard than any of their Western counterparts, while the mining operation was becoming barely profitable. When the next anti-exploitation strike broke out, the capitalists cried to the Soviet government for help.

Bukharin, on behalf of the party and the government, answered that he had no power over the unions. This

119

was not a capitalist country where governments oppressed their workers. This was a workers' state, ruled by the workers who were getting angry at capitalist exploitation, and the government had to obey their will. Long story short, and not necessarily in these words, the gist of the message was that the Brits only had Stalin's mercy standing between them and the pitchforks, and they better not push it.

Finally the Brits fathomed the depth of the hole they'd dug themselves into. There was nothing else they could do except run away from the threat of the pitchforks as fast as they could. Shipping back the equipment would only increase their losses, so they left the machinery behind.

As a result, the Soviet government got new working equipment, trained workers, and well-organized production - all free of charge. None of the captains of socialist industry lost any sleep; it was done for the common good of the workers, and so the end justified the means. According to a witness account, members of the party's central committee, including Stalin, laughed hysterically every time Bukharin retold the story of how the workers' state fooled Western capitalism.

But the joke really was on the workers. As soon as the British left, the mines were taken over by the state, the wages dropped to the national average, and the usual misery ensued. The unions had done their job; there were no more strikes. Who would dare protest the party that acted in the interests of the workers? No one was foolish enough to stick his head into that noose and be declared enemy of the people. And since everyone acted smart and in the interests of the common good, the industry quickly declined to the pre-capitalist level.

In 1937, Bukharin himself was declared an enemy of the people and, after a show trial, executed on unrelated charges. The allegations against him were as bogus and far-fetched as the very system he had helped to create - and of which he later became a victim. The gold-mining episode was perhaps one of the most innocent schemes he conjured in the interests of the common good.

"We asked for freedom of the press, thought, and civil liberties in the past because we were in the opposition and needed these liberties to conquer. Now that we have conquered, there is no longer any need for such civil liberties."
- Bukharin, 1917

In the absence of economic incentives, the stagnant and unproductive industries could only be run by threats and intimidation. Those who think that the Soviet system was an aberration of socialism, consider that it had been consistent with the principles of equality and the common good. Stalin's reign of terror was merely an inevitable end result of a collectivist utopian theory that contradicted human nature, vilifying people for "greed" and "selfishness," which were mere manifestations of their individuality, and punishing the desire to be free from state-run slavery.

It appears that the ultimate manifestation of the "common good" principle is an absolute power of the state. Stalinists associated the idea of "socialism with a human face" with moral confusion and ideological corruption. At least the henchmen were consistent in their beliefs.

As post-Stalin liberal reforms softened the totalitarian system, they also made it more dysfunctional. With the fear of repressions withering away, the economy slowed down to a halt. And just as the last remaining fear was gone in the years of Perestroika, the country fell apart.

This was a logical conclusion of an attempt to build a "workers' paradise" based on "progressive" collectivist morality, which turned workers into slaves and corrupted the society to such an extent that it required a partial return of totalitarian rule by Putin in order to rein in organized crime.

But American "progressives" seem to be unable to learn from other people's mistakes, even if the former KGB officer Vladimir Putin himself is asking Obama to take a lesson from the pages of Russian history and not exercise "excessive intervention in economic activity and blind faith in the state's omnipotence."

I don't often agree with Putin, but when he's right, he's right. "In the 20th century, the Soviet Union made the state's role absolute," he said at the World Economic Forum in Davos. "In the long run, this made the Soviet economy totally uncompetitive. This lesson cost us dearly. I am sure nobody wants to see it repeated."

About the Author

Oleg Atbashian, a writer and graphic artist from Ukraine, currently lives in New York. In the USSR he was a teacher, a translator, a worker, a freelance journalist, and at one time a propaganda artist, creating visual agitprop for the local Party committee in a Siberian town. He moved to the United States in 1994, hoping to forget about politics and enjoy life in a country that was ruled by reason and common sense, whose citizens were appreciative of constitutional rights, the rule of law, and the prosperity of free market capitalism. But what he found was a society deeply infected by the left-ist disease of "progressivism" that was jeopardizing real societal progress. The result is this book, as well as many more essays, political parodies, and cartoons, published in various media in America and around the world. Most of it is collected at his satirical website ThePeoplesCube.com - a spoof of "progressive" ideolo-gy, which Rush Limbaugh described on his show as "a Stalinist version of the Onion."

About "Shakedown Socialism"

"Oleg Atbashian has written a timely warning for Americans about the collectivists among us and their plans for the future. I hope everyone reads this book."

-- David Horowitz
Author of *Uncivil Wars* (2003);
The Professors: the 101 Most Dangerous Academics in America(2006); ***Indoctrination U.*** (2008); and most recently ***One Party Classroom*** (2009)

"Ayn Rand saw it coming: 'When government controls are introduced into a free economy, they create economic dislocations, hardships and problems, which -- if the controls are not repealed -- necessitate further controls, which necessitate still further controls, etc.' In his brilliant, witty, and wonderfully illustrated **Shakedown Socialism**, Oleg Atbashian -- who grew up in the Soviet Union, shows how that process is happening in Obama's America today, and explains why that is putting us on the road to ruin. **Shakedown Socialism** is an enlightening, sobering, and wonderfully clear explanation of why statism kills -- and thus also of why and how Barack Obama is killing the American economy. Oleg quotes Putin saying that when the Soviets made the state's role absolute, the U.S.S.R. became completely economically uncompetitive, and no one wants to see that repeated. No one except Obama, that is. This book shows why Obama's statist economic policies are a looming disaster for America and for the spirit of the free human individual."

-- *Pamela Geller*,
*author, **The Post-American Presidency: The Obama Administration's War On America***

"Brightly written and filled with entertaining and illuminating illustrations, Oleg Atbashian's **Shakedown Socialism** is a clear and eye-opening guide to exactly what is wrong with socialism and state control of the means of production, and how it kills both the economy and human initiative. Atbashian saw it all up close in the Soviet Union, and now he sees Barack Obama making the same mistakes -- and sounds this clarion call for economic sanity, before it's too late. **Shakedown Socialism** is an essential and inspiring guide to the virtues of the free market."

*-- **Robert Spencer**,*
*author of the New York Times bestsellers **The Politically Incorrect Guide to Islam (and the Crusades)** and **The Truth About Muhammad***